CONSUMERGUIDE®

QUICK FIXES

Gardening Basics

pil Publications International, Ltd.

Picture credits:

Brand-X: 5, 15 (top), 78; **Getty Images:** 79; **iStockphoto:** 21, 28, 29, 32 (bottom), 33, 50, 67, 74 (top), 75 (top), 77; **Jklune:** 37; **Jerry Pavia:** 52 (center), 57 (top), 63 (top), 65; **PhotoDisc:** 6, 12 (bottom), 17 (top), 22, 23 (top), 56; **Photos.com:** 40; **Jack Schiffer:** 8; **Shutterstock:** 4, 26 (bottom), 30 (bottom), 38, 44 (bottom), 45 (top), 57 (bottom), 58, 64, 68 (bottom), 69, 71; **Carol Simowitz:** 63 (bottom)

Contributing Illustrators: Taylor Bruce, Marlene Hill Donnelly

Louis Weber, CEO
Publications International, Ltd.
7373 North Cicero Avenue
Lincolnwood, Illinois 60712

ISBN-13: 978-1-4127-8254-8
ISBN-10: 1-4127-8254-6

CONTENTS

CREATING A GARDEN

Have you always dreamed of starting a garden of your own but were never quite sure where to begin? Or perhaps you are interested in improving your existing landscape but need a few helpful hints? Whether you're a gardening novice or a seasoned pro, *Quick Fixes: Gardening Basics* contains the practical advice you'll need to minimize your efforts and maximize your results.

This book begins with the fundamentals: soil, water, and light. We'll give you the dirt on how to ensure great rewards at bloom time. Perhaps a soil test is necessary to determine whether you should adjust the nutrients in the soil, or maybe you need to switch the time of day that you're watering your plants. Our tips will help you get your garden off to a great start.

We'll also discuss simple strategies to keep your garden looking great. Learn the ins and outs of maintenance and pruning, discover how to prevent pests and diseases, and explore the ways organic gardening can add to the ease and enjoyment of tending to your yard.

Once you've covered the basics, you can begin to outline your landscape plans. With a little planning and our helpful hints, you can create a landscape filled with flowers and greenery. Short on time and/or space? Check out our low-maintenance gardening techniques for ideas to maximize both.

Well, what are you waiting for? Dig in!

CHAPTER ONE

GETTING STARTED

To succeed in cultivation, most plants need good soil with suitable drainage and texture. They also need moisture and light to keep them healthy and thriving. These basics provide an important foundation for any yard or garden, and with our helpful hints, you'll be sure to get off to a good start. The tips included here will help you enhance your landscape—and maybe even your enjoyment of gardening.

THE DIRT ON SOIL

Good soil is the first step to a great garden. The loose, dark earth of the fabulous gardens seen on television and in magazines doesn't usually just happen. It is created by gardeners improving their native soils. Soils can be amended with sand to make them looser and drier or with clay to make them moister and firmer. They can be given plentiful doses of organic material—old leaves, ground-up twigs, rotted livestock manure, and old lawn clippings—to improve texture and structure. Organic matter nourishes any kind of soil, which, in turn, encourages better plant growth.

Before you start to plant, make sure your soil has been thoroughly prepared.

Start with the Right Plants

Use plants adapted to the conditions right outside your door. When plants prefer your native soil and climate—

no matter how difficult these conditions may be—they are more likely to grow beautifully with little effort. Native plants—shade trees, shrubs, or flowers that arise in the nearby countryside—are good options. Or, try less common plants from faraway places with conditions similar to your own.

- To identify suitable plants, begin by identifying your garden conditions. Have your soil tested or do your own tests (see pages 8–12) to determine if you have a light and sandy soil, a moderate and productive soil, or a heavy clay soil.

- Watch the site to see how sunny it is, and select plants accordingly.

- Find your location on the United States Department of Agriculture hardiness zone map (see page 80), which indicates average minimum winter temperature.

- Make a note of the light levels, soil conditions, and climatic zone information you've found. Then check nursery catalogs and gardening books to find plants that thrive in every one of the elements particular to your yard. Use these plants as a shopping list for all your future gardening projects. A little extra legwork in the beginning makes gardening much easier over the coming years.

- Look for the tales weeds have to tell as they grow in your garden. Weeds are opportunists, taking advantage of any vacant soil to make their home. (Just think of how well this strategy has benefited the dandelion, a native of Eurasia that has swept through America.) Although they seem to grow everywhere, dandelions prefer fertile, often heavy soil. Likewise, other weeds favor certain kinds of soil. Acidic soil can encourage the growth of crabgrass, plantains, sheep sorrel, and horsetails. Alkaline soil (also called *sweet* or *basic* soil) is favored by chamomile and goosefoot. Fertile, near-neutral soils can provide a nurturing environment for redroot pigweed, chickweed, dandelions, and wild mustard.

- Even if you can't tell one weed from another, you can find out important information by looking at them closely. If a vacant garden area has few weeds taking advantage of the opening, the soil is likely to need plenty of work. If weeds are growing, but only sparsely, and have short, stunted stems and discolored leaves, the area may have a nutrient deficiency, and a soil test is in order. If, in newly tilled soil, weeds sprout up quickly in certain areas and more slowly in others, the weedy areas are likely to be moister and better for seed germination.

Soil Testing

Get a soil test before you start adding fertilizers and amendments to your garden soil. This follows the old advice, "If it ain't broke, don't fix it." Sometimes unnecessary tampering with nutrients or soil acidity can actually create more problems than benefits.

- Soil tests tell you the nutrient levels in your soil, a plant version of the nutrient guides on packaged foods. They also note pH and organic content, two factors important to overall smooth sailing from the ground up.

A soil test will help you identify whether your soil needs amending.

- To have your soil tested, call your local

Cooperative Extension Service, often listed under state or county government in the phone book. Ask them how to get a soil-testing kit, which contains a soil-collecting bag and instructions. Follow the directions precisely for accurate results. The results may come as a chart full of numbers, which can be a little intimidating at first. But if you look carefully for the following, you can begin to interpret these numbers:

- If the percentage of organic matter is under 5 percent, the garden needs some extra compost.

  Nutrients will be listed separately, possibly in parts per million. Sometimes they are also rated as available in high, medium, or low levels. If an element or two comes in on the low side, you'll want to add a fertilizer that replaces what's lacking. Add only the nutrients your soil test says are necessary.

Some Sources of Specific Nutrients

Many of these fertilizers are available processed and packaged.

Nitrogen: livestock manure (composted), bat guano, chicken manure, fish emulsion, blood meal, kelp meal, cottonseed meal

Phosphorus: bonemeal, rock phosphate, super phosphate

Potassium: granite meal, sulfate of potash, greensand, wood ashes, seabird guano, shrimp shell meal

Calcium: bonemeal, limestone, eggshells, wood ashes, oyster shells, chelated calcium

Boron: manure, borax, chelated boron

Copper: chelated copper

Magnesium: Epsom salts, dolomitic limestone, chelated magnesium

Sulfur: sulfur, solubor, iron sulfate, zinc sulfate

Zinc: zinc sulfate, chelated zinc

- Soil pH refers to the acidity of the soil. Ratings below 7 are acidic soils. From 6 to 7 are slightly acidic—the most fertile pH range. Above 7 is alkaline or basic soil, which can become problematic above pH 8. Excessively acidic and alkaline soils can be treated to make them more moderate and productive.

pH Levels

It is always best to choose plants that thrive in the pH of your existing soil. If you must alter the pH of your soil, follow the guidelines below.

- Use ground limestone to raise the pH of acidic soils. Limestone is nature's soil sweetener, capable of neutralizing overly acidic soils. It's best to add limestone in the fall to allow time for it to begin to dissolve and do its job.

  The amount of limestone you use will vary depending on the specific soil conditions. Simple home test kits, or a professional test, can be used to determine the soil's pH. If you dump limestone on soil randomly, you run the risk of overdosing the soil. Follow guidelines on the limestone package or on a soil test.

- To lower the alkalinity and increase the fertility of limey and other soils with very high pH, add cottonseed meal, sulfur, pine bark, compost, or pine needles. These soil amendments gradually acidify the soil while improving its texture. Garden sulfur is a reliable cure when added as recommended in a soil test. It acidifies the soil slowly as microbes convert the sulfur to sulfuric acid and other compounds.

- Maintaining the new and improved pH is an ongoing project. Recheck the soil's pH every year and continue to add amendments as needed.

Texture Checkup

Check the texture of your soil in a jar filled with water. This test is simple to do at home and provides important information about your soil.

- Gather some soil from the garden, choosing a sample from near the surface and down to a depth of 8 inches. If you have dry clay, pulverize it into fine granules, and mix well. Put a 1-inch layer (a little over a cup) in a quart glass jar with ¼ teaspoon powdered dishwasher detergent. (Dishwasher detergent won't foam up.) Add enough water to fill the jar ⅔ full. Shake the jar for a minute, turning it upside down as needed to get all the soil off the bottom, then put the jar on a counter where it can sit undisturbed.

- One minute later, mark the level of settled particles on the jar with a crayon or wax pencil. This is sand. Five minutes later, mark the amount of silt that has settled out. After another hour or so, the clay will slowly settle out and allow you to take the final measurement. These measurements show the relative percentages of sand, silt, and clay—the texture of your soil.

  - Soil that has a high percentage of sand (70 percent or more) tends to be well aerated, ready to plant earlier in spring. But it also tends to need more frequent watering and fertilization than heavier soils.

  - Soil that has 35 percent or more clay retains moisture well, so it takes longer to dry in spring and may need less watering in summer. It can be richer and is more likely to produce lush growth with just the addition of compost and, occasionally, a little fertilizer. The compost is important. It helps break up clay so the soil won't be too dense and poorly aerated.

  - Soil that has nearly equal percentages of sand, silt, and clay can have intermediate characteristics and is generally well suited for good gardening.

Testing Drainage

Test your soil's drainage by digging a hole, filling it with water, and watching how quickly the water disappears. All the soil tests in the world won't do a better job than this simple project. It tells you how quickly moisture moves through the soil and whether the soil is likely to be excessively dry or very soggy—neither of which is ideal.

- When it hasn't rained for a week or more and the soil is dry, dig several holes that are 1 foot deep and 2 feet wide. Fill them to the top with water and keep track of how long it takes for the holes to empty. Compare your findings to the following scale:

  - 1 to 12 minutes: The soil is sharply drained and likely to be dry.

  - 12 to 30 minutes: The soil has ideal drainage.

  - 30 minutes to 4 hours: Drainage is slow but adequate for plants that thrive in moist soil.

  - Over 4 hours: Drainage is poor and needs help.

Soil Amendments

Designated paths, such as this stone walkway, allow you to move through the garden without compacting the soil and planting beds.

Once you know the nature of your soil, it's easy to amend it to meet the needs of the plants you want to grow.

- Add a thick layer of mulch and let it rot to improve the soil of existing gardens. Minerals, released as the mulch is degraded into nutrient soup, soak down into the soil and fertilize existing plants. Humic acid, another product of decay, clumps together small particles of clay to make a lighter soil. For best success, remember these points:

  - Woody mulch, such as shredded bark, uses nitrogen as it decays. Apply extra nitrogen to prevent the decay process from consuming soil nitrogen that plants need for growth.

  - Don't apply fine-textured mulches, like grass clippings, in thick layers that can mat down and smother the soil.

  - Use mulch, which helps keep the soil moist, in well-drained areas that won't become soggy or turn into breeding grounds for plant-eating slugs and snails.

Sources of Organic Matter

Compost
Livestock manure
Straw
Grass clippings
Salt hay
Shredded bark
Bark chunks
Shredded leaves
Seedless weeds
Peat moss
Kitchen vegetable scraps
Mushroom compost
Agricultural remains, such as peanut hulls, rice hulls, or ground corncobs

- Get local compost from your city or town hall service department. Made from leaves and grass clippings collected as a public service, the compost may be free or at least reasonably priced for local residents. To find other large-scale composters, check with the nearest Cooperative Extension Service; they are up-to-date on these matters. Or try landscapers and nurseries, who may compost fall leaves or stable leftovers for their customers; and bulk soil dealers, who may sell straight

compost or premium top-soil blended with compost. Don't give up. Yard scraps are discouraged or banned in many American land-fills, so someone near you may be composting them.

- Plan ahead for bulky organic soil amendments—compost, manure, and leaves—that may be added by the wheelbarrow-load to improve the soil. This will raise the soil level, at least temporarily. As the organic matter decays, the soil level will lower.

  - If soils rich in organic matter drop to expose the top of a newly planted shrub or tree roots, add more soil or organic matter to keep the roots under cover.

  - If your garden is beside a house or fence, keep the soil level low enough so it won't come in contact with wooden siding or fencing that isn't rot-resistant.

  - When planting around existing trees, shrubs, and perennial flowers, avoid covering the crown—where stems emerge from the ground—with organic material. This helps prevent disease.

- Test your soil by feel before and after it is amended to judge the extent of the change. Take a small handful of lightly moist soil from several inches below the soil

Composting

Making your own compost takes several months, so many garden-ers find it easier to purchase bagged compost. Either way, compost is a good additive for soils low in organic materials. Added to clay soil, compost lightens the soil and improves aeration; added to sandy soil, compost can improve water-holding capacity.

surface. Squeeze it into a ball in your hand and watch the results when you extend your fingers. Sandy soils, which can have a scratchy feel, will fall apart. To enrich a sandy soil, apply and incorporate a several-inch layer of compost and even an inch or two of clay, then try again. When the soil is improved, the ball will cling together better.

Clay soils, which have a slick feel, will form a tight ball that's not easily broken up. To lighten clay soil, add

Soil that has equal percentages of sand, silt, and clay probably won't need amending.

extra compost and coarse sand. When the soil is light enough, the ball will break up with a tap of a finger.

- Till or spade a thick layer of compost into lightly moist (never wet) soil to bring it to life before planting a new garden. If you are starting with hard, compacted soil, it's necessary to spade the soil first to break it up. Go over the area, removing weed roots and other unwanted vegetation as you go. Then go over the soil with a rototiller.

After the first pass, go over it again crosswise until you break the soil into reasonably small pieces. If your soil is especially poor, see information on double-digging below.

Your well-tilled soil, like screened topsoil, may look great at first, but silt or clay soils are likely to get stiff, crusty, and hard after a few heavy downpours. The best way to keep soil loose and light is to add organic matter.

Add a 4- to 6-inch-deep layer (more if soil is very poor) of compost to the soil and work it down until it's 10 to 12 inches deep. The soil will become darker, moister, and spongier—a dramatic conversion right before your eyes. As long as the organic matter remains in the soil, the soil is likely to stay loose. But since it slowly decays, you will have to continue to add organic matter—compost, mulch, or shredded leaves—to maintain the desired texture.

• Try spading or no-till systems to preserve the texture and organic content of thriving garden soils. Once the soil is loose, light, and rich, minimal disturbance helps preserve the levels of organic matter. Avoid repeated tilling, which breaks healthy soil clumps and speeds up decay.

Instead of tilling, loosen rich soil before planting by turning the surface shallowly with a shovel and breaking it apart with a smack from the shovel backside. Very loose soil can be made ready for direct seeding by combing it with a hoe or cultivator.

Double-Digging

Double-digging garden beds to make high-performance gardens for deep-rooted plants such as roses and perennials is a tradition in many beautiful British gardens. The average rototiller works the soil only 8 or 10 inches deep and won't break up compacted soil below. Double-digging will.

- Double-digging requires a stiff upper lip, because it takes a lot of manual labor. Do a little at a time so you don't overdo it, or hire a professional landscaper if you have health restrictions.

- Start with vacant soil that is stripped of grass and other vegetation. Beginning at one end of the garden, remove a strip of soil a spade's length deep and a spade's width wide. Put it in a wheelbarrow. Use your shovel to turn the soil below it (likely to be one of the heaviest parts of the job) and break it up.

Double-dig a garden bed intended for deep-rooted plants such as roses.

Another (sometimes easier) option is to jab a garden fork (like a big pitchfork) into the hard lower soil and rock it around until the soil breaks up. If organic matter is needed, you should add it to the lower level at this point.

- Do the same thing to the second strip of soil next to the first row. This time, turn the surface topsoil into the first trench, adding organic matter as desired. Then loosen and amend the exposed subsurface soil. Continue filling each trench from the adjacent row and loosening the soil below. Fill the final strip with the soil from the wheelbarrow.

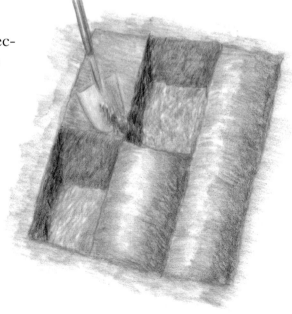

Raised Beds

Build raised beds where the soil is too hard, rocky, poor, or wet for plants to grow well. Instead of struggling to change these bad conditions, construct a great garden bed over them.

Time-saving Tip

Pile dug-out earth on a tarp instead of on the grass when digging a hole for planting or when excavating a garden pool. You can easily drag away any excess soil, and you won't have to rake up little clods trapped in the turf. Don't waste that soil. You can use it to fill a raised bed for herbs or vegetables.

In vegetable gardens, simply mound up planting rows 6 to 8 inches high and 2 to 3 feet wide. (You can walk in the paths beside the planting rows without compressing the raised soil.) Set permanent and decorative gardens in handsome raised-bed frames built of timbers, logs, rocks, or bricks, which can vary from 4 inches to 4 feet high. Don't hesitate to ask for professional help with big building projects, which need strong structures if you want them to last.

SHEDDING SOME LIGHT ON LIGHT

Many plants, especially lawn grass, flowers, roses, vegetables, fruit trees, and conifers (needle-leaved evergreens) thrive in bright sun, which provides abundant energy for growth, flowering, and fruiting. But some plants, particularly those native to forests and glens, need shadier conditions. Learn the sun requirements of any plant you intend to grow so you can put it in the right place.

Assessing Light Conditions

• Watch how sunlight and shadows hit the ground to determine how much shade exists during the growing season under deciduous trees (those that drop their leaves in fall). This test helps you determine which shade-loving plants will thrive there.

- Full shade is found under thickly branched trees or evergreens. A garden that's located here will receive little or no direct sun and remain gloomily lit. Only a limited number of plants are suitable for this situation. You should choose flowers and ferns with evergreen leaves.

- Partial shade is found under trees that allow sunlight to penetrate through the canopy and dapple the ground throughout the day. A garden grown under a lightly branched honey locust tree would fall into this category. A larger selection of plants are capable of growing under these conditions than in full shade.

Some Plants for Shady Conditions

PLANTS FOR FULL SHADE:
- Ferns, pachysandra, barrenwort

PLANTS FOR PARTIAL SHADE:
- **Spring wildflowers:** trout lilies, bloodroot, bellworts, Solomon's seal
- **Shrubs:** rhododendrons, azaleas, hydrangea
- **Shade-loving perennials:** bleeding heart, hostas, mint, bergenia, sweet woodruff, astilbes
- **Annuals:** impatiens, browallia

PLANTS FOR LIGHT SHADE:
- **Annuals:** begonias, coleus, ageratum, sweet alyssum
- **Herbs:** basil, parsley, bee balm
- **Vegetables:** lettuce, spinach, arugula
- **Perennials:** daylilies, hostas, anemones, hardy geraniums, coral bells, lobelia

- Light shade is found in places where plants are in direct sun for a portion of the day. This might be found in a garden under mature trees with tall barren trunks. The sun can shine in under the high leafy canopies. Light-shade conditions also exist on the east or west side of a wall or building. Here you can grow many shade-loving plants as well as shade-

Some Plants for Sunny Conditions

- **Broad-Leaf Evergreens:** boxwood, holly, waxmyrtle
- **Conifers:** pines, spruces, firs, junipers, false cypress, yews, arborvitae
- **Trees:** maples, oaks, elms, magnolias, crab apples, hawthorns, apples, pears, peaches, plums
- **Shrubs:** roses, viburnum, potentilla, spirea, lilacs
- **Perennials:** yarrow, sea thrift, Shasta daisies, chrysanthemums, coreopsis, pinks, coneflowers, blanketflowers
- **Annuals:** portulaca, gazania, gerbera, marigolds, zinnias, dahlias
- **Herbs:** lavender, thyme, sage, rosemary

tolerant plants, which are sun-lovers capable of growing moderately well in light shade.

- Providing a minimum of 6 to 8 hours of direct sun a day is sufficient for most plants that need full sun. The term "full sun" doesn't actually mean plants must be in bright light every moment of the day, only most of the day. The minimum must be met, however, even during the shorter days of spring and fall for perennials, trees, and shrubs.

Sun Intensity

Consider differences in sun intensity when planting on the east and west side of shade-casting trees or buildings. Even if east- and west-facing sites receive the same number of hours of sun, they will not produce identical results.

- Gardens with an eastern exposure are illuminated with cool morning sun, then shaded in the afternoon. They are ideal locations for minimizing heat stress in southern climates or for plants such as rhododendrons that can burn in hot sun.

- Gardens with western exposure are shaded in the morning and drenched in hot sun in the afternoon. Sunburn, bleaching, and sometimes death of delicate leaves can result, especially in warm climates and when growing sensitive young or shade-loving plants. Afternoon sun can also cause brightly colored flowers to fade. However, the west side of a building is the ideal place for sun-loving and drought-tolerant plants.

Indoors

When growing potted plants indoors, supplement natural light with fluorescent or grow lights. Sometimes in winter the weather may be cloudy for days, even weeks. This creates problems for tropical plants, potted flowers, and even foliage plants that need light to remain healthy.

The solution is to hang a fluorescent shop light directly over your indoor plants. Special grow lights or full-spectrum bulbs (formulated to produce light wavelengths that plants need most) can be used in place of fluorescent bulbs for spectacular results

Indoor potted plants may require a supplemental light source.

with flowering plants. For extra-easy maintenance, plug the lights into an automatic timer, then set them to turn on for 14 to 16 hours a day and off again at night.

THE WAYS OF WATER

Without water, plants wilt and die. But too much water can be as bad for plants as not enough. If land plants are submerged in water for too long—even if just their roots are submerged—they may rot or drown from lack of oxygen.

Balancing plants' water needs is like having a healthful diet. Everything should be consumed in moderation. Provide your plants with enough water for good health, but don't flood them with it.

Watering Guidelines

How and when you water your plants can make a big difference.

- Apply water in the cool of the morning or evening when the wind is calm and water loss through evaporation is minimal.

- Avoid watering disease-susceptible plants at night. If water sits on plant foliage for hours, it can encourage fungal diseases to attack leaves, buds, flowers, and fruit. Plants susceptible to leaf spots, fruit rots, and flower blights are best watered in the morning, when the warming sun will quickly dry the leaves and discourage fungus development.

- Provide an inch of water a week for many plants and grasses. The idea is to keep the soil lightly moist and to prevent it from drying out completely, which would be damaging to most plants. But because plants don't always follow the rules, there are exceptions to this general guideline:

Plants to Water in the Morning, Not at Night	
Roses	Tomatoes
Apples	Cucumbers
Pears	Melons
Peaches	Beans
Plums	Begonias
Cherries	Geraniums
Grapes	Peonies
Strawberries	Dahlias
Raspberries	Chrysanthemums
Blackberries	

- More water may be necessary if you have hot weather, dry sandy soil, or crowded intensive plantings or containers.

- When the weather is cool, the plants are widely spaced, or the soil is heavy and moisture-retentive, less water may be required.

- Young or new plantings require more moisture at the soil surface to help their roots get established. You should water more often to accommodate their needs.

- Mature plantings with large root systems can be watered heavily and less often than younger plants. The moisture soaks deep into the soil and encourages the roots to thrive.

It's best to water grapes in the morning so that fruit clusters dry out during the day.

- Set a rain gauge in an open area of the garden to learn how much water the garden receives each week. You can purchase an inexpensive one at a garden center. After each rainfall, check the depth of the rain inside. A commercial rain gauge is calibrated and easy to read. Judge the need for supplemental irrigation accordingly.

Rain gauges are also helpful when trying to determine when you have watered enough with an overhead sprinkler. Since some sprinklers apply water unevenly (more up close and less farther out), you could set several rain gauges around the garden and compare the amount of moisture each one collects. If the readings vary widely, move the sprinkler more frequently or invest in a more efficient model.

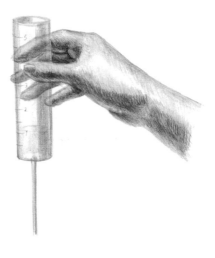

Hoses

- Stretch soaker hoses through the garden to provide water directly to plant roots. Soaker hoses are made of water-permeable fabrics, perforated recycled rubber, or other porous materials. When attached to a spigot with the water turned on low or medium, a soaker hose causes moisture droplets to weep out along its length. Very little evaporates and none sprays on plant foliage, helping discourage disease.

- Soaker hoses require a little special attention to work properly. Here are some hints:

  - Soaker hoses work best at low pressure (10psi). If you have high pressure, consider a pressure regulator or flow reducer for optimal performance.

  - Run soaker hoses straight through the garden. If set to turn or curve too sharply, they will kink and won't fill with water.

  - Expect more water to be released from the far end of the hose and less to be released from the closest end.

  - If the hose is moistening only one side of a plant root system, move the hose to water the dry side before you consider the job done.

  - To determine if the soil has been watered enough, dig into the soil beside the hose. If the water has seeped 12 inches down, it's about time to turn off the hose. Remember how long this took for the next time around.

- For faster results, look for flat hoses that are peppered with small holes. Of course there's a trade-off: These hoses do provide water more quickly, but they are not as gentle on the soil.

- If you like soaker hose results, you can upgrade to permanent or semipermanent drip irrigation systems. Although more expensive, these systems are custom-designed for varying soil types and individual plant water needs. They also don't need to be shuffled around the garden.

• Wheel hose carts around the yard instead of dragging armloads of hoses and causing wear and tear on your back. Hose carts consist of a reel with a crank that you can use to neatly coil the hose, eliminating tangles, knots, and kinks. This reel is set on a two- or four-wheeled base with a handle for easy pulling. Look for large-wheeled types if you're rolling the cart over the lawn or rough ground. Smaller wheels are fine on a paved path or patio.

• Place hose guides at the edges of garden beds to keep the hose from crushing nearby plants when you pull it taut. Hose guides, such as a wooden stake pounded into the ground at an outward angle, prevent the hose from sliding into the garden. Decorative hose guides (stakes carved like animals, elves, or flowers) can be found at some garden centers, mail-order garden suppliers, or craft shows. You could also improvise by using things like plastic pink flamingos, garden statues, or birdbaths.

• Use a water breaker on the end of your hose to change heavy water flow into a gentle sprinkle. This helps prevent soil compaction and spread the water more evenly across planting areas. Put an adjustable spray nozzle on the end of the hose, watering only with the setting that produces fine droplets in a gentle spray and wide arc. Save the strong blasts for washing the car.

Or, look for spray heads developed specifically for garden use. Some are set on angled bases, making it easy to reach in between plants. Others are on long poles for watering hanging baskets.

Water breakers should be put on watering cans, too, especially when watering seedlings, which can be broken or uprooted with a strong drenching.

Conserving Water

• Use gray water on potted plants or small gardens to reduce water use. Gray water is the leftover tap water from activities such as rinsing vegetables at the kitchen sink. Be sure to avoid water contaminated with water-softener salts, harsh detergents, fats, oils, or other extras that would harm plants.

• Catch water from a downspout in a container. This unfluoridated, unchlorinated water is ideal for watering plants. The easiest way

Grouping water-loving plants together looks beautiful and natural and makes your job easier.

to collect downspout runoff is to put a container at the bottom of the downspout. A topless bucket or barrel with a sturdy spigot at the bottom can be set in place permanently. Simply drain the water from the spigot into your watering can. To handle larger quantities of water, look for a 30- to 50-gallon barrel or drum. It's helpful to keep a large cup or other dipper on hand for transferring the water into a watering can. Be sure to cap containers so that birds, small mammals, and reptiles do not fall in and drown.

- Another option is to redirect runoff from downspouts into flower beds or lawns. Simply connect flexible tubing to the end of the downspout and direct it into nearby plantings around the foundation of the house or to flower or vegetable gardens. For maximum benefits, shape beds like a shallow bowl to collect the water and give it time to soak in. Or, as an alternative, the garden could be made fairly level with lower moisture-gathering saucers dug around newly planted trees or shrubs or plants with high moisture needs.

Moisture-Loving Plants

Louisiana, Siberian, and Japanese irises
Foamflowers
Marsh marigolds
Solomon's seal
Sweet flag
Horsetails
Swamp hibiscus
Cardinal flower
Impatiens
Hostas
Ferns
Joe-pye weed
Astilbes
Umbrella plant
Ligularia
Mint
Cordgrass
Willows

In dry climates, the tubing can be covered with soil or mulch and kept connected all the time. In climates with periods of overly wet weather, the tubing should be disconnected during soggy seasons to prevent oversaturation of the soil, which may cause plants to rot, unless you are growing water-loving plants such as Siberian iris.

CHAPTER TWO

GARDEN CARE

Keeping your garden looking great depends on having quality equipment, developing a good technique, and being organized enough to do the right things at the right times. This may sound like a lot to juggle, but once you understand the basics, it's easy.

MAINTENANCE AND PRUNING

Garden Tools

For a start, you'll need good hoes, spades, rakes, pruners, and a sturdy wheelbarrow. Buy the best tools you can afford. There is no substitute for good tools.

- One way to ensure good quality is to buy tools from a reputable dealer willing to guarantee their performance. For another quality test, look at the way tools are made. Tools with steel blades are strong enough to last for years without bending. Stainless steel is even better, because it won't rust. Spades, shovels, and forks with hard ash

Once your garden soil is in good condition, small hand tools are right for many tasks.

handles are unlikely to splinter or break in the middle of a heavy operation.

- Hand pruning shears are used for small stems under about a half-inch in diameter. Look for scissor-type blades, which make sharper, cleaner cuts than the anvil type with a sharp blade pressing on a flat blade. Also check out new ergonomically designed pruning shears that minimize repetitive motion stress. There are even shears made especially for left-handed gardeners.

- Loppers are long-handled pruning shears with larger blades for cutting branches up to about 1½ inches in diameter. Pruning is easier if you buy a model with ratcheting action for more power with less effort.

Invest in good gardening tools now to avoid headaches later.

- Pruning saws should have narrow blades, be easy to maneuver into tight spaces, and be toothed on one side only.

- People with smaller builds can find specially designed tools with smaller blades and shorter handles, which are easier to control than oversized tools.

- Keep hand tools in a basket on the garage or pantry shelf so they are always easy to find. Nothing is more frustrating than seeing a branch in need of a quick trim but having to search all over the

Keep small maintenance tasks simple—hand tools stored in a basket are always accessible and are easy to transport.

house and garage for a pair of pruning shears. If all your tools are kept together—and returned to their proper place after each use—simple garden projects will stay quick and uncomplicated.

- To keep tools upright and organized, attach a topless and bottomless coffee can or similarly shaped plastic container to the top of a fence post, securing it with wire. You can slip in the handles of rakes, shovels, and hoes, keeping them together and out from underfoot.

- Keep a bucket of clean sand and machine oil in the garage to cure tools after each use. This is particularly helpful for rust-prone digging instruments such as shovels, garden forks, and hoes. After use, rinse tools with water and dry the blades. Then insert them in the oil/sand mixture before you put them away. The sand will scour off debris, and the oil will coat the metal, retarding rust.

Mulching

Cover garden beds with a layer of mulch to keep weeds down and reduce the need for water. Annual weed seeds are less likely to sprout when the soil is covered with enough mulch to keep the surface in the dark.

Many annual weeds germinate in autumn, so keep your soil mulched all season.

When it comes to water, even a thin layer of mulch—nature's moisturizer—will reduce evap-

oration from the soil surface. Thicker mulches can reduce
water use by as much as 50 percent.

- Mulches vary in their appearance, makeup, and texture,
  which will influence how you use them. Here are some
  examples:

  - Varying appearances: For a
    soothing, natural-looking garden,
    use dark-colored organic mulches
    made of bark or compost. For
    a brilliant-looking garden,
    consider a mulch of bright gravel.
    In utilitarian gardens such as
    vegetable gardens, straw makes
    an excellent mulch. Avoid colored
    mulch or beauty bark.

  - Soil improvement: This calls for the use of organic
    mulches that break down to add organic matter to the
    soil.

  - Texture: For maximum effectiveness with only a thin
    mulch layer, look for fine-textured mulches such as
    twice-shredded bark, compost, or cocoa hulls. For
    an airy mulch, try thicker layers of coarse-textured
    mulches such as straw or bark chunks.

- Kill off sod or dense weeds by layering newspaper, alone
  or with a thick layer of compost or mulch, directly on
  the garden site. This treatment cuts off the sunlight to
  unwanted vegetation, which will eventually decay and
  add organic matter to the garden. The newspaper decom-
  poses, too. (What a bargain!)

- Mulch new plants with straw or chopped leaves after
  planting in the fall to prevent root damage during winter.
  A little mulch used immediately after planting can help to
  keep the soil moist and encourage continued root growth.

But the main reason to mulch lies ahead, in winter. Alternately freezing and thawing, expanding and contracting soil can break new roots or even push new plantings out of the ground, a process called *frost heaving.* By mulching generously with an airy material like straw when the soil first freezes, you can help keep the soil frozen until winter ends, at which point the mulch can be removed.

- In winter, mulch evergreen perennials and ground covers with evergreen boughs to protect them from winter burn (the cold-weather opposite of sunburn). When the soil is frozen, the wind is strong, and the sun is bright, moisture is pulled out of the vulnerable leaves and cannot be replaced by the frozen roots. A  protective layer of evergreen boughs, possibly obtained by recycling the branches of a Christmas tree, forms a protective shield over vulnerable greenery. Straw will also do the job, especially in colder areas where there is less chance of rot in winter.

Pruning

A few basic pruning cuts will help you rejuvenate and control the size of your shrubs and trees. Prune with top-quality pruning shears, loppers, and a saw. Sharp blades and sturdy handles can make pruning a breeze. Dull blades that are rusty and sticking make projects

Hand pruning shears work well on smaller stems.

harder than they need to be. They can also cause wood to be crushed or torn, which is damaging to the plant. Look for hard, durable blades capable of being resharpened and a sturdy, smoothly operating nut holding the blades together. Hand shears should also have a safety latch to keep the blades closed when not in use.

- Candle-prune pines to control their size or make them branch more thickly. Candle-pruning (also called *candling*) refers to manipulating the candle-shape new shoots that arise in spring. When the candle is fully elongated but before the needles enlarge, use your pruning shears to cut off a little, half, or most of the soft candle, depending on how much you want to limit size. The cut should slant at an angle instead of slicing straight across the candle. Come the following spring, clusters of new side branches will appear. Continue candling each year for more dramatic results.

  Candling is especially handy for keeping mugo pines small enough for use near the house or in a mixed border. It also can help lanky, open-branched pines fill in to form a more solid and substantial cone.

- Renewal-prune flowering shrubs by removing one-third of the stems once each year. This modest effort acts like a fountain of youth, keeping these shrubs young. It's much better than shearing, which reduces flowering, has to be repeated frequently, and can even accelerate aging.

Use pruning loppers or a pruning saw to cut the

Spring-blooming shrubs such as rhododendron can be pruned after they finish blooming.

oldest stems off at the ground, ideally in early spring before the shrubs break dormancy. This timing encourages
quick renewal, but a few spring flowers will be sacrificed
on early bloomers. If you can't bear that thought, wait to
prune until after flowering. As spring and summer prog-
ress, new branches will take the place of the old branches.
If pruned every year, the shrub will be continually rejuve-
nated, remaining healthy and beautiful.

- Rejuvenate tired,
  overgrown, or weak
  shrubs by cut-
  ting them to the
  ground. Although
  this may sound
  like giving up, just
  the opposite is
  true. It can be the
  start of a whole new shrub. This technique works well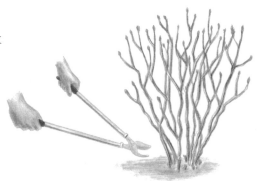
  with easy-growing shrubs such as lilacs, viburnums, and
  butterfly bushes but is generally not effective with evergreen shrubs (except boxwoods). The idea is similar to
  renewal-pruning, only more radical. It should be done in
  early spring before leaves or flowers emerge. Shrubs with
  strong root systems will resprout with a fountain of new
  stems. So that they don't crowd each other, you should
  thin excessively thick clumps to allow the strongest to
  continue growing and form the foundation for the new
  shrub.

  Shrubs with weak root systems or disease problems may
  not resprout. If there are no signs of life a month or two
  after cutting the shrub back, start looking for a replacement plant.

- Prune to the outside of a tree's branch collar for fast heal-
  ing and good tree health. The branch collar is the swell-

ing located at the base of the branch, where it arises from another limb or the trunk. The branch collar is like a hospital isolation ward; it houses protective chemicals that help keep diseases from invading the parent limb. When removing a branch for any reason, leaving that branch collar in place shuts out any passing pathogens.

- Slant pruning cuts away from the bud to encourage water to run off. This helps keep the bud healthy so it can grow and prosper.

Staking

Use wire grid supports instead of individual stakes to easily hold up bushy but floppy perennials such as peonies. You can buy commercial grid supports, which are handsome round or square grids neatly set on legs. Green grids are more camouflaged amid the foliage than metallic grids. Or you can make your own grid supports out of a sheet of wire mesh, cut a little wider than the plant it will support. The extra length can be bent into legs.

The supporting process takes one simple step. Set the grid over a newly emerging perennial in spring. The stems will grow up through it, retaining their natural shape while staying firmly upright.

The alternative (which occurs when you let the plant sprawl before staking it) is more difficult

Perennials that Often Need Support

Asters

Balloon flowers

Bellflowers (taller types)

Garden phlox

Hollyhocks

Foxgloves

Pyrethrum daisies

Sedums (taller types)

Shasta daisies

Yarrows

and less attractive. Corsetting the drooping limbs with twine and hoisting them up with a stake of wood can result in broken stems and a miserable-looking specimen.

PESTS AND OTHER PROBLEMS

Preventing Disease

Growing healthy plants is the first step toward a great garden. To achieve this, it's important to prevent disease by paying careful attention to plant selection, planting, and care.

- Choose disease-resistant cultivars whenever possible. They are bred to resist infection—an ideal way to avoid diseases. Growing disease-resistant vegetables prevents chemical tainting of your food. Disease-resistant varieties of popular flowers save you time, trouble, and expense.

There are varying levels of protection available:

Some Disease-Resistant Cultivars

Apples: 'Liberty,' 'Jonafree,' 'MacFree,' 'Freedom'

Beans: 'Florence,' 'Buttercrisp,' 'Jade'

Cucumbers: 'Park's All-Season Burpless Hybrid,' 'Fancipack,' 'Homemade Pickles,' 'Tasty King,' 'Sweet Success,' 'Salad Bush'

Peas: 'Super Sugar Snap,' 'Sugar Pop,' 'Maestro,' 'Green Arrow'

Roses: 'The Fairy,' 'Red Fairy,' rugosa roses, 'Carefree Delight,' David Austin English Roses, Town and Country Roses, Meidiland roses

Strawberries: 'Surecrop,' 'Cavendish,' 'Redchief,' 'Allstar,' 'Guardian,' 'Scott,' 'Lateglow,' 'Delite'

Tomatoes: 'Celebrity,' 'Better Boy,' 'LaRossa,' 'Enchantment,' 'Sunmaster,' 'Mountain Delight,' 'Big Beef,' 'Beefmaster,' 'Sweet Million,' 'Viva Italia,' 'Roma'

- Some cultivars have multiple disease resistances for maximum protection.

- Some cultivars resist only one disease. But if that disease is a problem in your area, then these plants will be worth their weight in gold.

- Other plants are disease-tolerant, meaning they may still get the disease but should grow well despite it.

• Spray plants susceptible to foliage fungus with wilt-proofing solution before disease strikes. This product is a pine oil modified to spread into a film coating that protects evergreen foliage from drying out during winter. An unexpected side effect of the film is that it keeps fungus spores from penetrating into susceptible leaves. Mix according to label directions and try it on phlox, bee balm, cucumbers, watermelons, tomatoes, and apples.

Pair disease-resistant varieties with good garden practices to reduce pest and disease problems.

• Experiment with baking soda sprays to prevent fungal diseases. Mix 2 teaspoons baking soda in 2 quarts water with ½ teaspoon corn oil. Shake well, put in a sprayer, and go to work. Spray susceptible plants often and always after rain to prevent diseases such as powdery mildew.

• Thin the stems of disease-prone plants to improve air circulation. Mildew-susceptible phlox and bee balm, for instance, can grow into clumps so thick that they block airflow. This encourages fungus attack, but it is easily corrected. When new growth is coming up in the spring, cut out every third stem, targeting those that are weak or in areas of the thickest growth.

Preventing Pests

- Interplant herbs and flowers with vegetables to help reduce pest problems. This gives the vegetable garden a colorful patchwork look and helps confuse problem pests. The varied aromas of interplantings make it hard for pests to find their favorite food by scent. This works particularly well if you interplant with powerfully fragrant herbs and flowers such as mints, basils, lemon geraniums, garlic, or onions.

- Attract beneficial insects. Sprinkling flowering plants amid the garden helps draw ladybugs, spiders, lacewings,

Ladybugs are beneficial insects.

and tiny parasitic wasps who prey on plant-eating pests. The flowers provide shelter plus nectar and pollen, an alternative food source.

Once beneficial insects are at home in your garden, keep them there. Remember, they can be killed as quickly as plant pests by broad-spectrum pesticides, which kill indiscriminately. It's best to avoid pesticides or use targeted pesticides such as Bt (a bacterial disease of caterpillars that won't harm other insects) to protect beneficial insects.

- Use floating row covers to keep pests off vegetables. This simple idea works rather well. Floating row covers are lightweight fabrics that you can drape over plants. They allow sun, rain, and fresh air to penetrate, but if secured to the ground with rocks, bricks, or long metal staples, they will keep flying insects out.

- Use barriers of copper strips or diatomaceous earth to keep slugs away from plants. Slugs are voracious plant eaters. They eat almost anything, ganging up on tender succulent plants and eating them down to the ground.

They thrive where soils are damp, spending sunny days under rocks, logs, or mulch and coming out to eat when it's rainy or cool and dark. Any slug-control measures you use will work better if you clear out excess mulch and any dark, dank hiding places where slugs might breed.

- Diatomaceous earth is a gritty substance that pierces the skin of soft-bodied slugs. Sprinkle it on the soil, encircling plants plagued by slugs. Use horticultural-grade diatomaceous earth, not the kind sold in swimming pool stores.

- Copper strips, set around the edge of the garden, prevent slug trespass by creating an unpleasant reaction when touched with the mucus on the crawling slugs. Set copper strips an inch deep and several inches high, so that slugs can't get over or under.

• Kill existing slugs by trapping them in deep saucers of beer. Slugs love beer, and that can be their downfall. Bury an empty plastic margarine tub in the garden soil. The top rim should be level with the soil surface. Fill the tub with beer (any kind will do) and leave it overnight. The slugs will crawl in and drown. Empty the tub every day or two and refill with beer until the tub comes through the night empty.

• Spray aphids off plants with a strong stream of water. Aphids, small sap-sucking insects with soft, pear-shape bodies, cling to succulent young stems and buds. They reproduce quickly, sometimes covering stems that curl and distort in protest. Because aphids can multiply into swarms almost overnight, it's important to eliminate any that you find. This method works best on mature

or woody plants that won't be damaged by the force of the water blast. Repeat every couple of days or any time you see new aphids arriving.

• Deer can be a nuisance in the garden. They seem to enjoy dining on cultivated plants and are worst in the winter, gobbling evergreens when their native food supply dwindles. But they are also a problem in spring and summer, when they like to munch tender flowers and new growth. In fall, males rub their antlers on wood and can damage small trees and shrubs.

This deer may look cute, but it's a nuisance in the garden.

Deer don't enjoy strong-smelling soaps and human hair so this is one way to repel them. Simply stuff powerfully scented soap in a mesh bag and dangle it from branches about 3 feet high. You also can set soap bars directly on the ground. Replenish the soap supply frequently so it won't dissolve away or lose its smell. You can also fill mesh bags with human hair. Hang them outside (like a furry scarecrow) so deer wonder if you are hiding in the garden. Refill bags as soon as you pull another handful from your hairbrush. If deer are a chronic problem, consider spraying plants with deterrents or erecting a fence.

ORGANIC GARDENING TECHNIQUES

Organic gardeners shun the use of synthetic chemicals to keep their yards free from potential hazards. But the real success of organic gardens lies in the methods used to keep plants growing vigorously, without a heavy reliance on sprays. Organic gardening cuts right to the heart of the matter: soil.

Soil is the life force of the garden. When enriched with organic matter, the soil becomes moist, fertile, and fria-ble—ideal for healthy plants. It also nourishes a rich population of beneficial organisms such as earthworms and nutrient-releasing bacteria. And it harbors root-extending fungi that help make growing conditions optimal.

- Make compost the lazy way by layering leaves, lawn clippings, and kitchen waste. Then simply leave it until it's ready. Nature's recyclers will take organic matter no matter how it is presented and turn it into rich, dark compost. This process just takes longer in an untended pile.

To begin your compost heap, dump yard scraps in a far corner of the yard. An ideal blend would be equal amounts of soft or green material (manure and fresh leaves) and brown or hard material (dead leaves and chopped twigs). Or, if you prefer, keep the compost materials neatly contained in a wooden-slat or wire-mesh bin. If you put an access door on the bottom of the bin, you can scoop out the finished compost at the bottom while the rest is still decaying.

- Add compost starter or good garden soil to a new compost pile to help jump-start the decay of organic materials.

Compost Blends

Organic material decays most quickly if blended with approximately equal parts of the following:

NITROGEN-RICH SOFT AND GREEN MATERIAL

- Manure from chickens, cows, horses, rabbits, pigs, guinea pigs, and other herbivores
- Fruit and vegetable peels
- Grass clippings
- Green leaves
- Strips of turf
- Alfalfa

CARBON-RICH BROWN AND HARD MATERIAL

- Wood chips
- Ground-up twigs
- Sawdust
- Pruning scraps
- Autumn leaves
- Straw

Compost starter, available in garden centers or from mail-order garden catalogs, contains decay-causing microorganisms. Some brands also contain nutrients, enzymes, hormones, and other stimulants that help decomposers work as fast as possible. Special formulations can be particularly helpful for hard-to-compost woody material like wood chips and sawdust or for quick decay of brown leaves.

Optional Compost-Making Equipment

- Wire composting bin
- Stackable composting bin
- Wooden composting bin
- Vented plastic bins
- Worm boxes
- Compost tumbler
- Compost inoculant
- Garden fork
- Compost thermometer
- Sifting screen

Good garden or woodland soil, although not as high-tech nor as expensive as compost starter, contains native decomposers well able to tackle a compost pile. Sprinkle it among the yard scraps as you are building the pile.

- Use perforated PVC pipes to aerate compost piles. An ideal compost pile will reach three to four feet high—big enough to get warm from the heat of decay. Why is heat important? High temperatures—when a pile is warm enough to steam on a cool morning—semi-sterilize the developing compost, killing disease spores, hibernating pests, and weed seeds.

But the problem is that for decomposers to work efficiently enough to create heat, they need plenty of air—and not just at the surface of the pile. Aeration is traditionally provided by fluffing or turning the pile with a pitchfork, which can be hard work. But with a little advance planning and a perforated pipe, this can be avoided.

Start a compost pile on a bed of branched sticks that will allow air to rise from below. Add a perforated pipe in the center, building layers of old leaves, grass clippings, and other garden leftovers around it. The air will flow through the pipe into the compost pile.

- Use on-site composting for easy soil improvement. Gather up old leaves, livestock manure, and/ or green vegetable scraps and let them lie in or beside the garden until they rot, then work them into the soil. Or just heap them on the garden in the fall and till them into the soil. They will be decayed by spring. You can also dig a hole, dump in the yard waste, cover it with a little soil, and let it rot in privacy.

- Expect to use more organic fertilizer, by volume, than synthetic chemical fertilizers. That's because organic fertilizers contain fewer nutrients by weight, averaging from 1 to about 6 or 7 percent. Contrast this with an inorganic lawn fertilizer that may contain up to 30 percent nitrogen, more than four times as much as organic fertilizer.

More is not always better when it comes to fertilizers. Lower-dose organic fertilizers are unlikely to burn plant roots or cause nutrient overdoses. Many forms release their components slowly, providing a long-term nutrient supply instead of one intense nutrient blast. Organic fertilizers may also provide a spectrum of lesser nutrients, even enzymes and hormones that can benefit growth.

For details on how to use fertilizers properly, read the package labels. The volume of fertilizer required may vary depending on the kind of plant being fertilized and the time of year.

• Use fish emulsion fertilizer to encourage a burst of growth from new plantings, potted flowers and vegetables, or anything that is growing a little too sluggishly for your taste. High-nitrogen fish emulsion dissolves in water and is easily absorbed and put to immediate use by the plant. For best results, follow the package directions.

• Add toad houses to the garden to attract toads for natural pest control. Ordinary toads become plant protectors just by hopping into the garden. They may not be pretty, but toads eat plenty of bugs, so you'll be glad to see them. To encourage toads to come to live in your garden, try the following:

▪ Put several broken clay pots in the garden for toads to hide under.

▪ Water when the ground gets dry to keep the environment pleasant for amphibians.

▪ Avoid spraying toxic chemicals on the garden.

▪ Watch out for toads when tilling, hoeing, shoveling, or mowing.

• Use organic repellents to chase away rodents and deer. Sprays made out of hot peppers, coyote or bobcat urine, rotten eggs, bonemeal, or bloodmeal—even castor oil—can make your garden

Rabbits nibble on the succulent stems of many perennials and shrubs. Use repellent sprays to deter them.

plants unappetizing to herbivores. Reapply the repellents frequently, and always after rain, to maintain high protection levels.

- Grow French or American marigolds to kill any nematodes in the garden soil. Nematodes—microscopic worm-like pests that can damage tomatoes, potatoes, and other crops—are killed by chemicals that are released by marigold roots and decaying foliage. You can plant marigolds in and around other nematode-susceptible plants. Or just till marigolds into the soil and let them decay before planting.

Plant French marigolds to rid your garden of nematodes.

PROPAGATION

Starting your own plants from seeds, cuttings, and divisions saves money and expands options. But be prepared to give propagation a certain amount of attention. Young plants need tender loving care to get them off to a good start.

Division of Perennials

Daylilies, hostas, astilbes, or other clump-forming perennials are easily divided with a sharp shovel. Just slice off an edge of the clump in spring or late summer. Uproot it and replant elsewhere. Keep the new division watered for at least several weeks or until it has regenerated lost roots.

Divide a large perennial clump into small divisions to get many little plants fast. This is a quick and easy way to make enough plants for the big drifts, clumps, or ground covers that are so popular in landscaping today.

A mature bee balm clump might contain 50 rooted sprouts, each of which can be separated and grown into a new plant. Other easily divided perennials include asters, daylilies, yarrow, phlox, lady's mantle, salvia, coreopsis, hardy geraniums, irises, mint, thyme, oregano, and winter savory. Here's how to make smaller divisions:

- In spring or late summer, dig up the entire perennial plant clump and wash soil off the roots with a hose.

- If dividing in late summer, cut back the foliage by half, or more, if plants are tall and hard to handle.

- Use your hands to break rooted sprouts into individual pieces. If roots are too hard to work apart by hand, slice them free with a knife or pruning shears. Each section should contain at least one leafy sprout and one cluster of healthy roots.

- Replant very small divisions into pots of peat-based planting mix and tend them carefully until they get a little bigger. Larger divisions can go right back into the garden if kept moist until they become reestablished.

Plants from Seed

Many plants grow well from seeds, especially annual flowers, herbs, and vegetables. You can find dozens of new, rare, or old-fashioned varieties in seed catalogs that aren't available in the local nurseries. Seed sowing allows you to grow a few, dozens, or even hundreds of seedlings from a packet costing a dollar or two. Talk about economy!

- Keep a notebook, calendar, or advance planner to remind you when to plant seeds. For example, seeds such as tomatoes and peppers need to be planted six to eight weeks before the last spring frost, but squash and cucumbers need to be planted only three weeks before the last spring frost. It can be hard to remember everything (and squeeze it into your schedule) unless it's written down.

Direct sowing in the garden, following directions on the packet for timing and depth of planting, is an option for those without time or space to start plants indoors.

- Keep good propagation records to track how successful each operation has been and how the young plants are proceeding through the seasons. These records will guide you in future years. Jot down your observations weekly in a notebook. Or keep an index card on each plant you propagate so it's easy to find the next time. Some gardeners may want to computerize their records. Here are some things to note:

  - How long seedlings grew indoors before being transplanted outdoors and whether that timing allowed enough, too little, or too much time for a great performance outdoors.

  - When you planted seedlings outdoors and how well they responded to the weather conditions at that time.

  - When the first shoots of perennial flowers and herbs emerged in spring and were ready to divide.

Seedlings Indoors

- Instead of buying pots or cell packs, recycle household containers for starting seedlings indoors. Wash containers thoroughly with soapy water, then sterilize them with a solution of 1 part bleach to 10 parts water. Poke holes in the bottom to allow excess water to drain out.

- If starting seeds in a window, take extra care to maximize light. Use a south-facing window that will receive sun all day. It should not be blocked by a protruding roof overhang or an evergreen tree or shrub. Without a south-facing window, it's worth considering building a light garden:

Hang foil reflectors behind the flat to keep seedlings from leaning toward the sun. If the seedlings are sitting on a windowsill, make a tent of foil behind them, with the shiny side facing the seedlings. This will reflect sunlight and illuminate the dark side of the seedlings. They will grow much sturdier and straighter as a result. In climates with cloudy weather or homes without south-facing windows, sun may not be reliable enough. A light garden is an ideal solution.

- For compact, even growth, start seeds indoors under lights rather than in a window. Seedlings must have bright light from the moment they peer up out of the soil.

Set seedlings under a fluorescent shop light. You can place seedlings on a table or counter and suspend the shop light from the ceiling over them. Or you can set up three or four tiered light stands. You can adapt ordinary shelves by attaching lights to the bottoms of the shelves and placing growing trays below each light. Put the lights on a timer set to turn on for 14 hours a day and off again (one less job for you). You can't beat the results!

- Make a mini-greenhouse under lights with a clear plastic garment bag. This traps humidity near seedlings, helping to protect them from wilting.

  To cover nursery flats full of seedlings, bend two wire coat hangers into arches and prop them in the corners of the flat, one at each end. Work the plastic over the top of the hangers, and tuck the loose ends in below the flat.

  It's even easier to make a greenhouse cover for individual pots. Slide two sticks (short bamboo stakes work well) into opposite sides of the pot. Then top with the plastic and fold it under the pot to keep it secure.

- Start seeds or cuttings in an old aquarium or clear sweater box to keep humidity high. Aquariums or sweater boxes are permanent alternatives to more makeshift options. They are particularly good for cuttings that may need more overhead and rooting room than seedlings. To reuse these containers, wash them with soapy water, rinse, and sterilize with a solution of 1 part bleach to 10 parts water.

Seedlings Outdoors

- Sow perennial and wildflower seeds outdoors in raised beds or spacious nursery pots (the kind you get big flowers in at the nursery) and let nature get them ready to sprout. Hardy perennials and wildflowers often have a special defense called *dormancy* that keeps them from sprouting prematurely during a temporary midwinter thaw (which would be damaging when the frost returned). They require a certain amount of cold—or alternating freezing and thawing—to indicate when winter is truly over and spring has begun. The easiest way to accommodate the cold requirement is by putting them outdoors.

CHAPTER THREE
DESIGN DETAILS

A good landscape design plays many roles. It blends the house into the yard, making the entire property look good and increasing its value. Through the design of the landscape, you can create outdoor privacy with vine-covered trellises, hedges, fences, or informal clusters of plants that act like the walls of an outdoor room. Knowing the potential of each landscape element allows you to use them for the best effect, making the most of your home and garden.

YOUR LANDSCAPE PLAN

Mapping Things Out

A simple assessment of your landscape needs is your first step in planning your property. Make a list of the features you want to incorporate into your design. Then you can begin to find room for it all and start putting the elements in place.

Flower gardens provide color, beauty, bouquets for the house, and food for birds and butterflies.

• Draw a map of your property and decide where the new beds and plantings will go before you start buying and planting. The map needs to be to scale—an exact replica of your property in miniature. Many designers use a scale in which a quarter inch on the plan equals one foot in your yard. This scale usually provides enough room to show considerable detail but is likely to require the use of oversize paper so that everything will fit on one sheet.

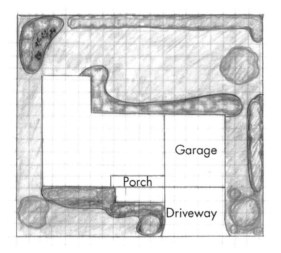

Measure the yard using a measuring tape (50-foot lengths work well), and sketch the perimeter on graph paper. Draw in existing trees, shrubs, fences, and other features you intend to keep, using an overhead view. Make some copies so you can experiment with designs. Then pencil in possible bed outlines and imagine how they will look. Once you've decided on the location of the beds, pencil in the plants you

Possible Landscape Features

SPATIAL/PRACTICAL:

- Barbecue area
- Children's play areas
- Dog pen and dog run
- Firewood storage
- Lawn for recreation
- Noise reduction
- Party or dance area
- Privacy
- Shade to keep home cooler
- Sitting/dining areas
- Soil retention for a bank
- Swimming pool
- Wind protection

OTHER CONSIDERATIONS:

- Berries for birds
- Eyesore screening
- Floral display
- Hobby gardening (water gardening, herb gardening, etc.)
- Vegetable garden

want to add (at the proper spacing) and get an accurate count of how many plants you'll need before you start shelling out any money.

- Plan the shape of the lawn, which is usually the biggest feature in a yard. The lawn's shape is more important than the shape of the beds. If it's designed with straight or gradually curving lines, the lawn can make a pretty picture and remain easy to mow. Avoid sharp turns, wiggly edges, and jagged corners, which are irritating to the eye and take extra work to mow.

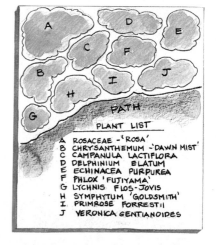

- Take photos and photocopy them. You can shoot the entire front yard or back-yard, the

A rounded lawn is pleasing to the eye.

plantings around the house's foundation, or individual gardens. Enlarge the images on a color copier, if one is available. Then you can sketch in prospective new plants and get an idea of how they will look. Winter is a great time to do this. Although the yard may be dormant, you won't forget how it usually looks.

- Borrow ideas from neighbors' gardens. There is no better way to learn what grows well in your area. You can also get great design ideas from other people. Remember, imitation is the sincerest form of flattery.

- Visit public gardens and nurseries with display beds for inspiration. These professionally designed gardens may have the newest plants and creative ideas for combining them. Look for gardens about the same size as your yard so you can apply what you learn directly.

Beds and Borders

- Make island beds half as wide as the distance from where you view them. Island beds, often oval or free-form, are situated in areas of lawn where they can be viewed from all sides. They may be near a corner of your yard or by your driveway or entrance walk.

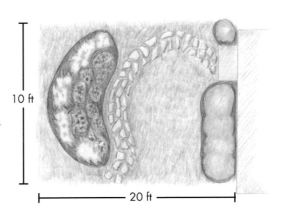

No matter where you put it, an island bed needs to be wide enough to look substantial from your house, patio, or kitchen window—wherever you usually are when you see it. A tiny garden located far from the house is more comical than beautiful. So, for example, if an island bed is 20 feet away, make it 10 feet across. In very large yards, keep beds closer to the house if you don't have time to maintain a large island bed.

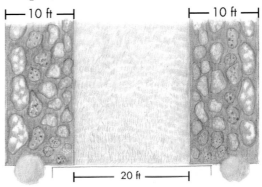

- Make borders up to half as wide as the total space in a small- or medium-size yard. For example, a 40-foot-wide yard could have one border 20 feet wide or two borders 10 feet wide. Borders—traditional gardens usually set at the edge of a yard, fence, or hedge—also need enough size to be in scale and make an impact in the yard. Wider borders can accommodate taller plants, including trees, shrubs, and large clumps of perennials and ornamental grasses, and so take on a rich diversity.

Paths and Pavings

Build garden paths anywhere that foot traffic wears out the grass. Paths make pleasing straight or curving lines through the yard and make it easier to get where you need to go in wet weather. They also save you the trouble of having to constantly reseed barren, foot-worn areas.

- Paving materials range in style, price, ease of installation and maintenance, and appearance. Here are four popular options:

  - Irregular flagstones create a casual but handsome appearance. The walkway is leveled and laid out more carefully on a gravel bed, with or without mortar. For a more formal appearance, rectangular stones are used.

  - Professionally laid brick paving is durable and rather formal. There are several possible patterns and edgings, but simpler styles look best. Paving bricks are flatter and

broader than bricks for buildings. Recycled or antique bricks can be used for paving and edging.

- An ordinary concrete sidewalk, plain and simple, is a good-looking and practical choice and is usually less expensive than stone or brick. Be sure to make the path sufficiently broad or it may look too cramped.

- Where a path is needed, and a casual look is desired, wood or bark chips can be used. This kind of path is permeable, so water does not run off, which makes it environmentally friendly. Because the chips break down, a new layer must be added from time to time to refresh the path. The old, decomposing chips can be left in place under the new ones or used for mulching or soil embellishments.

Garden Accents

- Use a collection of pots to end cut-throughs and shortcuts. Gaps in the shrubbery or fencing around your yard are an invitation for neighborhood kids to slip through. Even adults will be tempted to shortcut across the

lawn instead of following a longer path up the walk. Reroute traffic by blocking openings and detours with large pots of plants, flowers, herbs, or even your indoor floor plants brought outside in the summer. Cluster them together in a barrier that's not easily skirted. As a bonus, you'll have a dynamic plant grouping with maximum impact on the landscape.

- Create a shade garden without trees by planting under a vine-covered arbor. Shade gardens can feature serene blends of ferns, hostas, and woodland wildflowers, plus a few dazzling bloomers such as azaleas and rhododendrons. Although these plants usually grow amid trees and shrubs, they can thrive in shadows cast by other structures—walls, fences, houses, or a vine-covered arbor.

The advantage of an arbor shade garden is that fewer roots are competing for moisture and nutrients. And unlike a planting close to a wall or building, the arbor shade garden has plenty of fresh air circulation.

Vines for an Arbor

Clematis
Trumpet creeper
Trumpet honeysuckle
Climbing roses
Kiwi vine
Silver-lace vine
American wisteria

- Cover rocks and bricks with moss using a buttermilk-moss milk shake. A soft green moss veneer adds an air of antiquity, permanence, and beauty to walls, walks, or woodland rock gardens. You can wait a few years for moss to naturally creep into moist and shady places, or you can encourage a quicker appearance. Gather local cushion-forming mosses, the kinds that thrive in your climate, and find a garden location similar to where they naturally grow. Mix the moss with buttermilk in a blender and pour the concoction onto the appropri-

Cover rocks and bricks with a soft carpet of mosslike or low-growing ground covers.

Noise Reduction

Noise is a nuisance that limits garden enjoyment. Noise from the street or neighborhood is a common offender. Solid walls and dense foliage help block noise. Berms—mounds of dirt planted with shrubs and perennials—are good for deflecting noise; they also offer a sense of privacy.

ate rocks or bricks in your garden. Let it dry thoroughly. Keep the area moist, but not so wet that the milk shake washes off the bricks or stones. New moss will soon make an appearance.

- Reduce the volume of strong winds by planting a layered assortment of plants as a windbreak. Wind can knock down and dry out plants, generally making it harder to get the garden to grow well. Layered plants—taller trees with shade-tolerant shrubs planted under them—create an irregular barrier that gently stops wind. Solid fences, in contrast, allow wind to slip up and over and swirl back in on the other side.

- Plant bamboo for a quick and easy screen. Bamboo has handsome foliage and grows in upright thickets that can provide privacy. But most types of bamboo are vigorous spreaders. To keep them from overwhelming a garden, choose clump-forming types or plant them in large, submerged tubs or pots that keep the roots contained.

These midsize bamboo plants are attractive and provide privacy in the yard.

- Don't forget to place a bench in the garden. You can sit and admire your handiwork, which always looks best up close. Your bench, even a rugged one, can double as garden sculpture.

Attractive seating does double-duty here. It adds interest and charm to the garden while providing a comfortable place to enjoy the view!

Lawns

The emerald green lawn that spreads across most yards serves many purposes: It gives us places to play, filters air pollution, cools the air, and softens harsh light. But healthy, beautiful lawns don't just happen; they require work—more than just about any other part of the landscape.

If you're planting a new lawn and want it to be low-maintenance, choose the right kind of grass for the site, plant at the ideal time, and use organic and slow-releasing fertilizers. Or, if you're dealing with an existing lawn, follow our easy hints to minimize maintenance.

The grass strips here effectively widen the path.

- Use a mixture of turf grasses for a disease-resistant lawn. Diseases that attack one type of grass may not affect the others, so you are reducing the risk of problems.

- Grass blends also increase versatility. Fine fescues mixed with bluegrass, for instance, are less likely to turn brown in summer heat. Read the labels on lawn grass seed packages closely to identify which grass mixtures are used and how they might affect performance.

- Plant creeping red fescue in a lightly shaded lawn where bluegrass is likely to fail. For best results, provide well-drained, slightly acidic soil.

- Consider the merits of sod, seed, and plugs before choosing which to use to start a new lawn:

  - **Sod:** Sheets of prestarted turf can be purchased ready to be laid out on prepared soil, where they will take root and grow. Sod is expensive, but it provides an "instant lawn," and many people like that. It's great on a slope where grass seed can be washed away with the first heavy rain. But sod has a few potential problems in addition to its high cost. It may fail to thrive on difficult soils, and your selection can be limited to a few varieties and blends.

  - **Seed:** Grass seed is fairly inexpensive and available in a wide variety of custom mixes; there's something for every kind of lawn. It is best planted in cool, mild weather and must be kept constantly moist to germinate. The grass needs to become well established before summer heat or winter cold push it to the limits.

  - **Plugs:** These are small clumps of sod that can be planted like a ground cover in prepared soil. If kept moist and fertilized, the plugs will spread to form a solid sheet of turf. Plugs are an important way of starting warm-climate lawns and a way to economize in cooler climates.

Grasses for Different Purposes

COOL CLIMATES: SUN
Kentucky bluegrass

COOL CLIMATES: SUN OR LIGHT SHADE
Chewings fescue
Creeping red fescue

MODERATE CLIMATES: SUN OR LIGHT SHADE
Hard fescue
Tall fescue

WARM CLIMATES: SUN
Bermuda grass
Zoysia grass

WARM CLIMATES: SUN OR LIGHT SHADE
St. Augustine grass

BALL FIELDS
Perennial ryegrass

GOLF COURSES
Creeping bent grass

- Use seed rather than sod to establish grass on poor soils. Sod roots may never grow into stiff clay soils, which puts a damper on their future if drought strikes. Spend a little extra time and money to improve poor soil with compost. Then plant seed of suitable grasses and tend the lawn well (feeding, watering, raking, and weeding, as necessary) until it is growing steadily.

- Use edgings to keep grass out of garden beds. A physical barrier can prevent sprigs of grass from spreading to unwanted areas where they can make bed edges look ragged or spring up amid other plants.

Edgings made of 5- to 6-inch-wide strips of fiberglass, metal, or plastic—even stones or brick—can line the perimeter of a garden bed. Let the upper edge emerge a little above the soil (but well below the level of the mower) and the lower edge sink securely into the ground. More expensive edgings should last longer than cheap plastics, which can shift out of place during winter.

- Top-dress the lawn with compost or rotted manure to keep it healthy. Unlike super-concentrated fertilizers that stimulate rapid growth, these natural fertilizers provide light doses of nutrients and improve soil conditions. Make sure the compost

or manure is finely screened so it will settle down to the soil without packing on top of the turf.

- Fertilize lawns with slow-release nitrogen fertilizer. Slow-release products gradually emit moderate amounts of nitrogen over a period of weeks or months, so you won't need to fertilize as often. The nitrogen levels in slow-release products are high enough to keep your yard green and healthy, but not so high that the lawn is stimulated to grow rapidly and require continual mowing. Read fertilizer bag labels carefully to determine which brands contain slow-release nitrogen.

- Fill in low spots in uneven lawns by spreading sand evenly over the lawn area with a metal rake. You can sprinkle grass seed on the sand or you can wait for the surrounding grasses to send out new tillers and colonize the fill.

- Leave grass blades longer for more drought resistance and better root growth. Longer blades shade the soil and roots, keeping them cooler and moister, and the grass roots may grow deeper. In contrast, close-cropped lawns can dry out quickly in summer heat. The stubby blades expose grass-free openings where crabgrass and other weeds can grow.

- Keep your lawn mower blades sharp. Like a sharp razor on a day-old beard, your mower will slice through grass blades, giving a clean, level cut. Dull blades tear grasses, which can increase their susceptibility to diseases.

- Dethatch your lawn once a year or as needed to keep it healthy. Thatch is a layer of dead grass stalks that can build up at the soil surface, cutting off air, water, and fertilizer when it becomes thick and matted. Thatch can also harbor pests.

- A vigorous raking can help break up small amounts of thatch. For big problems, you can rent dethatching machines. Use them in mild weather and plan to reseed if necessary to refill gaps left behind. Once thatch is gone, the clippings can rot to enrich the soil.

- Don't mow the lawn during drought. Without rainfall, the grass is unlikely to grow much, if at all.

- Water sparingly during drought. Providing about a half inch of water every two weeks can keep grass alive without encouraging growth.

- Aerate compacted lawns to keep them healthy. With a lot of foot or wheel traffic, soil can become hard-packed, creating a poor environment for grass roots. To help air reach the roots (and also to cut out old thatch), run over the lawn with a core cultivator. This is a machine that pulls up small cylinders of soil, creating breathing spaces. Do-it-yourselfers can buy or rent a core cultivator (see the illustration on page 61). As an alternative, have a landscaper or lawn-care company core your yard.

- Try a fragrant herbal lawn for a change of pace. Herbal lawns release delightful fragrances when you walk on them or mow them. But few herbs will tolerate as much traffic as grass, so it's best to keep them out of the mainstream. You can blend low-growing creeping herbs into grass or plant a smaller area entirely in herbs.

- Consider mowing with a hand-powered reel mower. On a well-tended lawn, reel mowers provide an especially polished cut. They are also quiet and energy efficient.

Selecting Plants

Plant trees and shrubs first, then add flower gardens. Woody plants are the bones of the garden, the bold foundation that will be there summer and winter to enclose your yard or blend your house into the property. They are also the most expensive and permanent features and, as such, need to be given special priority. Plan well, find top-quality trees and shrubs, and plant them properly where they can thrive.

Variation in foliage can provide as much visual interest as flowers.

• Match the flowering plant to the site. Most flowers are high-performance plants, especially sensitive to inadequacies in light, moisture, soil, or other elements. Give them exactly what they need to thrive.

• Select flowering plants with a range of bloom times to keep the garden interesting through the seasons. Many perennials, shrubs, and trees will flower for a maximum of three weeks per year. On paper, list those that bloom in early and late spring, early and late summer, and early and late fall. Then when you plant your garden, you can develop a sequence so one kind of flower will fade as another begins to open.

Experiment with a mixture of warm and cool colors.

Annual flowers are great for filling the gaps. Pansies, sweet alyssum, and calendula thrive in cool spring and fall weather. Petunias, marigolds, zinnias, geraniums, and other annuals fill the summer months with color. And tender bulbs such as dahlias and cannas can also provide bright color through much of the warm summer season.

- Choose flowering plants with good foliage as well as flowers. The foliage will still be on display long after the flowers are gone. For starters, find plants with foliage that stays healthy, lush, and green and won't become off-colored, ragged, or diseased after flowering. Then you can expand to add plants with golden, silver, bronze, blue, or multicolored leaves that fit the garden color scheme.

- Use both warm and cool colors to give the garden just the right amount of emphasis. Warm colors such as yellow, orange, and red are bold and appear to be closer to you than they are. This makes them ideal for a garden located farther away from your house. Cool colors such as blue and purple recede from the eye and look farther away than they really

Perennials with Exceptionally Long Bloom

Purple coneflowers

Coreopsis

Rose mallow hibiscus

Lenten rose

Violet sage

Sedum 'Autumn Joy'

Asters

'Luxuriant' bleeding heart

Blanketflower

'Stella d'Oro' daylily

Russian sage

Stoke's aster

Pincushion flower

'Sunny Border Blue' veronica

Spiderwort

Mongolian aster

A weathered wheelbarrow adds a touch of country charm to this garden.

are. They make pleasant, quiet gardens close to the house, but they may be lost farther away.

You can blend cool and warm colors to give a feeling of movement and depth in the garden. Color blends also provide vivid contrast, which some people find particularly exhilarating.

• Consider varying leaf sizes for more design interest. Large leaves like those on hostas or oak leaf hydrangeas advance and stand out (similar to warm-colored flowers). They are striking in prominent locations, but if over-used they will lose their impact.

Small or finely textured leaves, as on thread leaf coreopsis or carrot tops, recede from the eye and look farther away. They can best be appreciated up close. Or if you are trying to make a garden look deeper, these variet-ies might be used toward the rear as a floral

Use plants with various leaf sizes for visual impact.

optical illusion. But when used exclusively, fine textured leaves may look busy and weedy.

• Add the impact of flower size to get another vari-able for an interesting design. Large flowers are bold and prominent. Smaller flowers and fine flower clusters recede. Blending airy, small flow-er sprays with large, bold flowers combines the best of both textures. Planting larger flowers toward the front of the garden and smaller flowers toward the rear increases visual depth.

Sneak Preview

If you're designing a flower bed and want the quickest possible preview of your combinations of color and shape, try using the color pictures from last year's seed catalogs to test your ideas. Cut out pictures of plants that interest you. Block out the bed on graph paper and try different pictures in different positions. When you find the combinations that work best for you, use them as a basis for your design.

CHAPTER FOUR

LOW-MAINTENANCE GARDENING

If you are used to cutting your lawn every week and shearing your shrubs once a month, you may be relieved to know that there are easier ways to keep your yard looking nice. Low-maintenance gardening begins with choosing plants ideally suited to your yard's conditions so they won't need coaxing to stay alive.

MINIMIZING UPKEEP

Trouble-Free Planting

Some plants are naturally easier to keep, requiring little but suitable soil and proper exposure to grow and prosper. You can plant them and let them be without worrying about pests and diseases or extensive pruning, watering, fertilizing, or staking. Spending a little time finding these easy-care plants will prevent hours of maintenance in coming years.

• Choose dwarf and slow-growing plants to eliminate the need for pruning and pinching. Tall shrubs just keep growing, and growing, and growing... sometimes getting too big for their place in the landscape. Lilacs, for example, commonly grow to 12 feet high. If planted by the house, they could cut off the view from a window. The only solution is regular trimming or replacement. A better option is to grow dwarf shrubs or special compact varieties that will only grow 2 to 4 feet high. They may never need pruning and won't have to be sheared into artificial globes.

Tall flowers and vegetables may not be able to support the weight of their flowers and fruit. They might need staking, caging, or support with a wire grid to keep them from falling flat on their faces. Flowers such as delphiniums, asters, and Shasta daisies are now available in compact sizes that are self-supporting. And shorter types of daylilies are less likely to become floppy in light shade than taller types. Compact peas and tomatoes, while not entirely self-supporting, can be allowed to grow loosely on their own, or they may need only small cages or supports to be held securely.

- Avoid fast-spreading and aggressive perennials such as yarrow, plume poppy, 'Silver King' artemisia, and bee balm. Although these plants are lovely, they have creeping stems that can spread through the garden, conquering more and more space and arising in the middle of neighboring plants. Keeping them contained in their own place requires

Bee balm can spread aggressively if it's not controlled.

Compact Shrubs for Foundation Planting

Dwarf balsam fir

Compact azaleas

Compact barberries

Compact boxwood

Heather

Compact false cypress

Cotoneasters

Daphne

Deutzia

Fothergilla

Hydrangea, French and oakleaf

Hypericum

Compact hollies

Compact junipers

Leucothoe

Mahonia

Dwarf Korean lilac

Dwarf spruce

Japanese andromeda

Mugo and other small pines

Potentilla

Pyracantha

Roses

Spirea

Stephanandra

Compact viburnums

dividing—digging up the plants and splitting them into smaller pieces for replanting. This may need to be done as often as once a year, so it's better to just avoid them.

- Avoid delicate plants such as delphiniums, garden phlox, and hollyhocks, which need extra care and staking. Although spectacular in bloom, these prima donnas require constant protection from pests and diseases, plus pampered, rich, moist soil and, often, staking to keep them from falling over. If you simply have to try one, look for compact and/or disease-resistant cultivars, which are easier to care for.

- Turn a low, moist spot into a bog garden for plants that need extra moisture. You can even excavate down a little to create a natural pond. Plant the moist banks with variegated cattails, sagittaria, bog primroses, marsh marigolds, and other moisture-loving plants.

Take advantage of wet soil by planting a bog garden.

Container Gardening

Containers are a great option if you're interested in low-maintenance gardening. There is no need to tolerate difficult soil or make do with marginal sites. You can start with any potting mix, picking the perfect blend for the plants you want to grow. You can set the pot where it will have

Group pots of annuals together for more visual impact.

the ideal amount of sun or shade. You provide water when nature comes up short, and you schedule the fertilization. There is nothing left to chance, assuming, of course, that you take the time to tend the potted plant. In return, containers become living flower arrangements. With lively color schemes, varied textures, and handsome containers, potted plants grow, flower, and flourish close at hand where they are easily enjoyed. Make sure the container is large enough to accommodate the root mass. Undersize containers need constant watering.

- Plant annuals in a big bag of potting soil for a quick, easy balcony garden. This method, commonly used in England, is still a novelty here and will make a great conversation piece:

  - Lay the bag flat on the ground where you want a mini garden. Punch a few small drainage holes in the bottom.

  - You can cut one large opening in the top side for several plants, letting them intermingle

Materials for Containers

Plastic

Clay

Ceramic

Fiberglass

Brass

Bronze

Tin

Stone

Cement

Cedar

Redwood

Compressed fibers

Compressed peat moss

in a decorative planting scheme. Or make several individual planting holes for a working garden of annual vegetables and herbs.

- The plastic wrapper will help to keep the soil inside moist. But when it does begin to dry out or needs fertilizer as a plant pick-me-up, carefully drizzle water or water-soluble fertilizer inside to moisten the entire bag.

- Use care when planting in decorative containers. Lovely bark, wicker, wood, and even fine pottery and urns make handsome containers. But some of them have one big drawback—they can be damaged by water. Regardless, you can still use them for plants, but only as an ornamental cover over a working pot below. Here is the trick:

- Plant in a plastic pot that has no drainage holes or that sits on a plastic saucer, which will prevent moisture spills.

- The pot, and saucer if used, must be smaller than the decorative container.

- Put a layer of plastic inside the container, then set the potted plant on top.

- Cover the top of the pots with sheet moss or other natural fibers to hide the mechanics below.

This combination will be temporary at best and require careful watering so the plant roots won't be drowned or dried. Once every couple of months, remove the potted plant and water thoroughly, draining off the excess moisture to wash out salts that will build in the soil.

- Sterilize old pots with a 10 percent bleach solution before using them for other plants. Saving old pots from flowers, vegetables, poinsettias, even shrubs transplanted into the yard is a great way to economize. But you have to be certain to eliminate any pests and diseases that may have come, like extra baggage, with the previous occupant.

Begin by washing out excess soil, bits of roots, and other debris with warm soapy water. Mix 1 part household bleach with 10 parts water and use the solution to wipe out the pot. Rinse again, and the pot is ready to plant.

Foliage Plants for Containers

These plants look great when they're mixed with flowering plants in pots:

- Caladiums
- Crotons
- Elephant ears
- Ferns
- Asparagus ferns
- Coleus
- Rex begonias
- Hostas
- New Zealand flax
- Scented geraniums
- Artemisias
- Spider plants
- Ivies

Use your imagination! This vintage baby carriage makes a charming and whimsical container.

- Create your own custom potting soil. Use a peat-moss-based potting mix as the foundation. (It works well for houseplants, seedlings, and many other plants as is.) Peat-based mixes won't compress like true soil, which is a big advantage in pots. But they are low on nutrients and liable to dry out quickly, complications that can be minimized with special potting blends.

  - To make a richer mix for annual flowers or for perennials like daylilies, you can blend 2 parts peat mix with 1 part compost.

  - For a more fertile, moisture-retentive soil for tomatoes or lettuce, blend 1 part peat mix, 1 part garden soil, and 1 part compost.

  - For a lighter mix for propagating cuttings or growing succulents or cacti, add 1 part coarse sand or perlite to 1 part peat mix.

- Premix a wheelbarrow full of potting blend. If you have plenty of house-plants that need repotting, or you like to put more than just a few pots or window boxes of summer flowers out-doors, this will save you time and effort. And if you buy the peat mix and extras in large, economy-size bags, it also will save you money.

- Premoisten peat-based mixes in a large tub or wheel-barrow. Prewetting peat moss, which soaks up a surpris-ingly large amount of water, ensures there will be enough moisture left over to supply new plantings.

Premoistening is easily done with a garden hose. Sprinkle in a generous amount of water, and work the moisture into the peat mix with a trowel (or a hoe if you are making large batches). Continue to add more water until the peat clumps together in a moist ball. Then it is ready to go in a pot. Don't let the mix get soggy.

- Place a circle of fine mesh screen over pot drainage holes instead of using pebbles or pot shards. The screen will help to hold the soil in place until the roots fill out and claim every particle. But it's still a good idea to water outdoors, in the sink, or over a pot saucer so a little oozing dampness or soil won't damage anything.

The problem with covering drainage holes with pot shards (the clay chunks left after a pot is broken) and pebbles is that they can shift to clog up the drainage holes. With no place for excess water to go, plant roots may soak in saturated soil, a condition few plants emerge from alive.

- Use water-holding gels to reduce the need for watering, especially when planting in quick-drying, peat-based mixes. These gels—actually polymers—look like crystals when dry and safely sealed in their package. But once you add water, you'll be surprised to see them swell into a large mass of quivering gelatin look-alikes. You can blend the gel into potting mixes, following blending instructions on the package.

- Use window boxes to brighten your house with flowers and add height to surrounding gardens.

If space is an issue, consider planting colorful arrangements of flowers in a window box.

- Elegant window boxes can feature flowers that match the color of nearby curtains, carpets, shrubs, or shutters.

- Some cascading ivy, vinca vine, or vining petunias will soften the geometric outlines of the window box.

- Grow herbs such as thyme, basil, and parsley in a kitchen window box.

• Set a narrow, perforated PVC pipe in the center of a strawberry pot or large container before filling in around it with potting mix. When you need to water your plants, run the hose gently into the pipe, and the water will ooze out from top to bottom, inside to outside, giving every plant an even share.

• Use slow-release fertilizers to keep plants growing and blooming all season. Because peat-based mixes contain little or no natural nutrients, plant growth depends on a regular supply of fertilizer. Slow-release fertilizers keep working for several months to a year, depending on the formulation.

- Seal the bottoms of clay saucers with polyurethane to keep them watertight. Then they will be safe to use on floors and carpets. Or, instead of buying clay saucers, you can buy watertight plastic saucers made to look like clay. When one is sitting beneath a pot, it's hard to tell the difference.

- Keep a succession of new flowers blooming in pots throughout the seasons, so your home and yard will never be short on color.

  - In spring, enjoy cool-season flowers like forced bulbs, primroses, and pansies.

  - In summer, grow tender perennials and annuals like impatiens and begonias.

Keep a watertight saucer, either clay or plastic, under flowerpots.

  - In fall, enjoy late bloomers like asters, mums, and ornamental grasses.

- Put clay and plastic pots in the garage before cold winter weather arrives. This will help keep them from cracking and chipping when the weather turns bitterly cold.

- Wrap heavy urns and pots that are too bulky to carry indoors in plastic for winter protection. Do this on a dry autumn day, securing the plastic across the top, bottom, and sides of the pots to prevent moisture from getting inside. Moisture expands when it freezes. This causes terra-cotta, ceramic, and even synthetic stone and concrete containers to chip and break.

- Store pots under a tarp for protection in mild climates. This will save space in your garage or basement and keep the pots handy for when you need them in the spring.

- Look for self-watering planters if you aren't home enough to keep potted plants from drying out (or if you forget to water every day or two). Self-watering planters have a water reservoir in the bottom that's connected to the pot by a water-absorbing wick. When the soil begins to get dry, the wick pulls up more water from the reservoir.

Reducing Maintenance

Selecting the right style of planting for any given area can also reduce maintenance. Instead of lawn grass that needs regular fertilizing, watering, and mowing, a self-sustaining meadow area can be appealing and leave you with plenty of time for your other interests. This and other tips will help your landscape look great with less effort.

- Plant weedy spots with thick-growing ground cover to avoid becoming a drudge to weeding. Ground cover works well on banks, in sun or shade, under fencing where it's hard to keep weeds down, beside outbuildings, and even under trees where it's too shady for grass to grow.

It's important to start the ground-cover bed in weed-free soil, however, so the ground cover can take over without competition. Another option is to clean up the soil. Turn it over with a rototiller or spade, let the weeds sprout, and then turn it again. Repeat the process until the weeds are almost gone.

Ground-cover plants are a low-maintenance option for shady areas where grass won't grow well.

Choose a ground cover that will thrive on the site. It needs to spread vigorously and grow thickly enough to crowd out any weeds. In shady areas, try pachysandra, barrenwort, or wild ginger. In sun, try creeping junipers, daylilies, ground-cover roses, or other plants that are specifically suited for your climate.

For good results fast, buy plenty of plants and space them relatively close together. If this is too expensive, spread plants farther apart, and mulch the open areas to discourage weeds. Plan to keep a close eye on the new garden for the first year and pull up or hoe down any weeds that appear. Water and fertilize as needed to get the ground-cover plants growing and spreading quickly. Once they've covered the soil solidly, there won't be any space for weeds.

Black-eyed Susans produce a wealth of summer flowers and will freely reseed themselves.

• In areas distant from the house, plant native meadow grasses and flowers that only need to be mowed once a year. Then have fun watching meadow garden flowers come and go throughout the season.

You can find seed mixes or prestarted turflike carpets of meadow plants specially blended for different regions of the country. To feature your location's unique meadow plants, just let the area grow wild, and meadow plants will come on their own. (Be sure to check with your local municipality before planting a meadow garden to be sure you won't be violating any ordinances. It's also wise to run the idea past your neighbors if your yard is visible from their yard.)

While they are getting started, newly planted meadows will need weeding and watering. Once in the late fall—after the flowers and grasses have all set seed—mow them down and let the seeds scatter to come up next year. Purchased wildflower carpets and mixes may contain colorful flowers that disappear after several years. You can sprinkle new seeds or plug in new clumps of a wildflower carpet to reintroduce them for color if you want.

- Mow down old flower stalks in late fall to clean up a flower garden. Before mowing anything but grass with your mower, make sure it has a safety feature that will prevent debris from being thrown out at you. Using suitable lawn mowers can save you plenty of time compared to cutting back the flower stalks by hand. If you allow the old stems to scatter around the garden instead of bagging them, you may find an abundance of self-sown seedlings arising in springtime.

Some Meadow Plants

Black-eyed Susan	Shasta daisy
Evening primrose	Snow-in-Summer
Coreopsis	Butterfly flower
Blanketflower	Maiden pinks
Native grass	Penstemon
Goldenrod	Rock cress
Sunflowers	Wild lupine
Aster	Gayfeather
Coneflower	

- Speed up the compost-making process by chopping up leaves and twigs before putting them on the compost pile. The smaller the pieces are, the faster they will decay. Chopping can easily be done with a chipper-shredder or a mulching mower.

Poppies make a colorful addition to any meadow garden.

USDA PLANT HARDINESS ZONE MAP

The United States Department of Agriculture Plant Hardiness Zone Map divides North America into 11 zones based on average minimum winter temperatures, with Zone 1 being the coldest and Zone 11 the warmest.

This map should only be used as a general guideline, since the lines of separation between zones are not as clear-cut as they appear. Plants recommended for one zone might do well in the southern part of the adjoining colder zone, as well as in neighboring warmer zones. Factors such as altitude, exposure to wind, proximity to a large body of water, and amount of available sunlight also contribute to a plant's winter hardiness. Because snow cover insulates plants, winters with little or no snow tend to be more damaging to marginally hardy varieties.

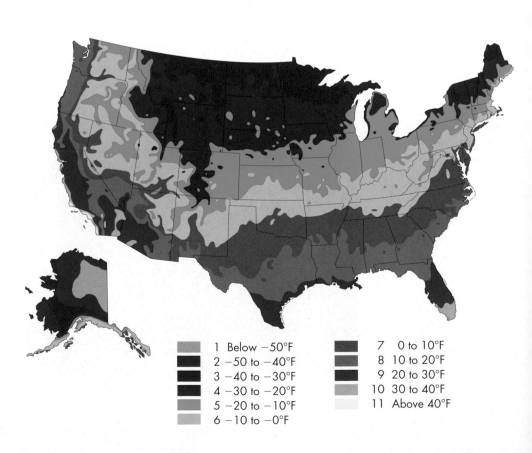

1	Below −50°F	7	0 to 10°F
2	−50 to −40°F	8	10 to 20°F
3	−40 to −30°F	9	20 to 30°F
4	−30 to −20°F	10	30 to 40°F
5	−20 to −10°F	11	Above 40°F
6	−10 to −0°F		